D1266353

MONUMENTAL MILESTONES
GREAT EVENTS OF MODERN TIMES

The Creation of Israel

Israelis pray at the Western Wall, the holiest Jewish religious site. The Islamic Dome of the Rock mosque rises behind it.

Mitchell Lane
PUBLISHERS

P.O. Box 196
Hockessin, Delaware 19707

Titles in the Series

The Creation of Israel

Russian Jews flee in terror from attacks by Christians. Some of them would settle in what is now Israel.

Jim Whiting

Printing   1   2   3   4   5   6   7   8   9

Library of Congress Cataloging-in-Publication Data
Whiting, Jim, 1943–
    The creation of Israel / by Jim Whiting.
        p. cm. — (Monumental milestones)
    Includes bibliographical references and index.
    ISBN-13: 978-1-58415-538-6 (library bound)
    1. Zionism—History—Juvenile literature. 2. Jewish-Arab relations—History—1917–1948—Juvenile literature. 3. Israel—History—20th century—Juvenile literature. 4. Balfour Declaration—Juvenile literature. I. Title.
DS149.W494 2008
956.8405'2—dc22

                                                                        200702319

ABOUT THE AUTHOR: Jim Whiting has been a remarkably versatile and accomplished journalist, writer, editor, and photographer for more than 30 years. He has long been fascinated by the circumstances surrounding the birth of Israel and has read numerous books on the subject. A voracious reader since early childhood, Mr. Whiting has written and edited more than 250 nonfiction children's books on a wide range of topics. He lives in Washington state with his wife and two teenage sons.

PHOTO CREDITS: Cover, pp. 38, 39, 40—Associated Press; p. 3—Hamburg Tourism Board; pp. 16, 13, 14—JupiterImages; p. 8—Barbara Marvis; p. 12—State Hermitage Museum of St. Petersburg, Russia; p. 19—Palestinian Academic Society for the Study of International Affairs; p. 24—National Archives; pp. 30, 36—AFP/Getty Images.

PUBLISHER'S NOTE: This story is based on the author's extensive research, which he believes to be accurate. Documentation of such research is contained on page 46.
    The internet sites referenced herein were active as of the publication date. Due to th fleeting nature of some web sites, we cannot guarantee they will all be active when you ar reading this book.

                                                                                PP

Contents

The Creation of Israel

Jim Whiting

*For Your Information

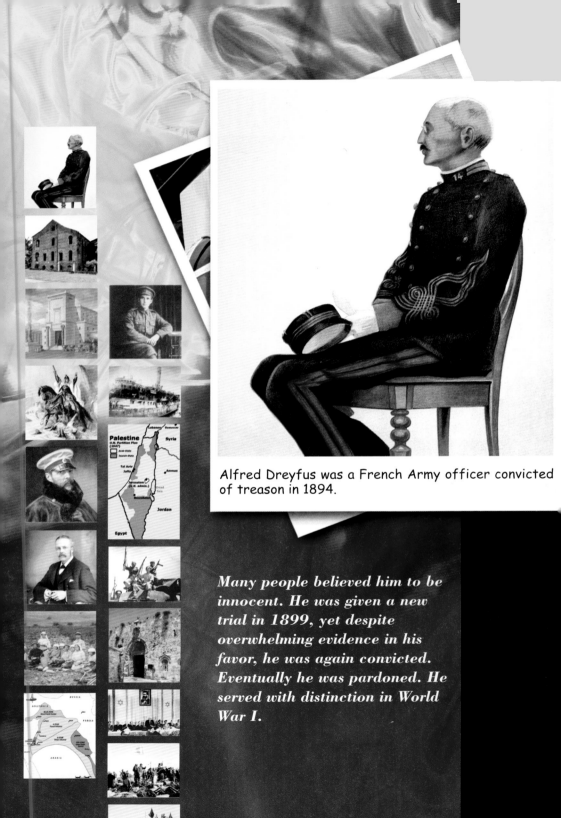

Alfred Dreyfus was a French Army officer convicted of treason in 1894.

Many people believed him to be innocent. He was given a new trial in 1899, yet despite overwhelming evidence in his favor, he was again convicted. Eventually he was pardoned. He served with distinction in World War I.

The Birth of Zionism

On a raw January day in 1895, French Army Captain Alfred Dreyfus stood at attention in the courtyard of the École Militaire, the French military academy. An officer ripped the buttons and insignia from Dreyfus's jacket, then broke Dreyfus's sword across his knee. Bystanders shouted, "Traitor!"

This public humiliation was designed to demean Dreyfus, who had been convicted late the previous year of spying for Germany, France's enemy. Several weeks later, a ship transported him to the notorious French prison of Devil's Island.

Under normal circumstances, Dreyfus would have died in obscurity. His circumstances, however, were hardly normal. It soon appeared that Dreyfus was innocent. His case generated a controversy that bitterly divided France before his name was cleared in 1906. Even then, it took nearly ninety years for the French Army to acknowledge its mistake. In 1995, General Jean-Louis Mourrut admitted that "the affair was a military conspiracy which ended in the deportation of an innocent man."[1]

There was one "crime" of which Dreyfus was definitely "guilty": He was Jewish. That was almost certainly why he had been punished in the first place. As *Time* magazine noted in 1995, "The Dreyfus case unleashed a political storm at the time. It sundered the French between such 'Dreyfusards' as the crusading writer Émile Zola who saw the young Captain as the innocent victim of an anti-Semitic [anti-Jewish] officer corps and traditionalists who regarded any attack on the army as unpatriotic. In fact, for some anti-Semitic groups, Dreyfus symbolized the supposed disloyalty of French Jews."[2]

Hordes of journalists covered Dreyfus's trial. One was Theodor Herzl, a Jew himself. To that point, Herzl had no interest in politics, though he knew that Jews in Europe had been persecuted for centuries. Like many other Jews, he believed in assimilation, the belief that at least in Western Europe, a more

Dreyfus was imprisoned on Devil's Island for several years.

Devil's Island is in the Atlantic Ocean, about seven miles off the coast of French Guiana. Escape was virtually impossible. The last of its prisoners was released in 1953.

enlightened age had done away with anti-Semitism and had welcomed Jews into its cultural and political fabric.

The intensity of anti-Semitism Herzl experienced as he stood next to French citizens screaming "Death to the Jews!"[3] convinced him that assimilation was a myth, that Jews would never be safe unless they had their own homeland: "the promised land, where we can have hooked noses, black or red beards . . . without being despised for it. Where we can live at last as free men on our own soil, and where we can die peacefully in our own fatherland."[4] He used his writing skills to produce a novel in 1896 called *Der Judenstaat* (The Jewish State).

The book struck a responsive chord. Under Herzl's leadership, the First Zionist Congress met in Basel, Switzerland, the following year. More than 200 delegates attended, with their deliberations focused on a proposed Jewish state. Herzl suggested Argentina, emphasizing its healthy climate, good soil, and relatively small population. However, it quickly became apparent there was only one location that met with general approval: Eretz Yisrael (Land of Israel). In this ancient Jewish homeland of Palestine, Jews had settled more than a millennium before the birth of Jesus in the belief that God had given the land to them. The name of the congress reflected this relationship: Zion was one of the names for Jerusalem, the longtime Jewish capital of Eretz Yisrael.

"Palestine is our unforgettable historic homeland," wrote Herzl. "The very name would be a marvelously effective rallying cry."[5]

This rallying cry was based on the history of the ancient Jewish kingdom. Founded around 1050 BCE, at its peak it stretched from the modern-day border of Israel and Egypt to the Euphrates River in Iraq. Its powerful leader, King David, conquered Jerusalem and made it his capital. David's son Solomon built the First Temple there.

After Solomon's death, the land became two kingdoms, Israel and Judah. Israel was conquered by the Assyrians in 721 BCE, while Judah fell to the Babylonians nearly a century and a half later. The temple was destroyed and nearly all the Jews were forced to move to Babylon.

King David wanted to build the temple, but, according to the Bible, God ordered him not to. David assembled all the materials, and his son Solomon constructed it in seven years. It stood for nearly 400 years.

An artist's conception of the First Temple in Jerusalem.

They returned several decades later and built the Second Temple, though they were ruled by foreign governments for nearly 400 years. Led by Judas Maccabee, they successfully revolted in 166 BCE and became independent. This victory is celebrated in the Festival of Lights, or Hanukkah.

About a century later, the expanding Roman Republic conquered Judea, as the Jewish land had become known. The Great Jewish Revolt that began in 66 CE was savagely suppressed, and countless numbers of Jews were killed or sold into slavery. The Romans destroyed Jerusalem and virtually all of the Second Temple, leaving only a single wall. It became known as the Western Wall (or Wailing Wall), the holiest Jewish site today.

Another revolt against Roman rule began in 132 and was put down. To prevent a recurrence, the Romans forced nearly all Jews to leave Judea in the Diaspora (meaning "scattered" or "exiled"). Only a handful remained. To stamp out the last traces of Jewish identity, the Romans renamed Judea as Syria Palestina. Coming from *Philistine*, the name of the ancient enemies of the Jews, the term was an intentional insult. Although they had been exiled, the land was always in Jewish memory, and many traditional prayers concluded with "Next year in Jerusalem."

The rise of Islam several centuries later allowed some Jews to realize those prayers. Islamic leaders encouraged Jewish settlement in Jerusalem. The settlement suffered in 1099 when Christian knights in the First Crusade captured Jerusalem and slaughtered nearly all the Muslims and Jews living there. The great Muslim leader Saladin regained Jerusalem in 1187, and the city remained under Muslim control for more than 700 years.

For most of this period, Jewish settlement in Palestine was sparse. Nearly all Jews lived in Europe, with strict limitations placed on their freedom of movement. In Western Europe, many lived in small, tightly packed neighborhoods that came to be known as ghettos.

The Jews were subjected to a great deal of prejudice. For example, historian Howard Sachar describes a cartoon carved into a ghetto wall in Frankfurt, Germany: "It revealed a trio of Jews debasing themselves around a sow. As one Jew suckled at the animal's teats, another (in rabbinical garb) lifted the *Judensau's* tail, allowing a third (also a rabbi) to drink the animal's excrement."[6] Nearby was an inscription alleging that a Christian baby had been ritually murdered by Jews, reflecting a common belief among Christians that the Jewish Passover ceremony demanded the blood of innocent Christians. Such beliefs encouraged Christians to periodically invade the ghettos and massacre many of the inhabitants.

Saladin recaptured Jerusalem and other areas in Palestine that the Christian Crusaders had taken nearly a century earlier. He was one of the few Muslims to be regarded with honor and respect among Christians.

Saladin was one of the greatest heroes of Islamic history.

Conditions were better in Spain, which was under Muslim control for several centuries. The Jews and Muslims were generally at peace. When Christians reclaimed control, however, they imposed their anti-Semitic outlook. In 1492, they forced most of the Jews to abandon their homes and live elsewhere.

After the Protestant Reformation, which began in 1517, the economy flourished. Jewish merchants and bankers became increasingly essential in Western Europe. Slowly their situation improved. As the nineteenth century progressed, it seemed that the worst of the horrors were over. Restrictions were lifted from the last ghetto, located in Rome, in 1870.

Conditions were different in Eastern Europe. Jews had to reside in the Pale of Settlement, an area established by Russian empress Catherine the Great in 1791. In this largely rural area, Jews lived in extreme poverty in villages and small towns known as *shtetls*. Eventually the Pale contained some five million Jews, nearly half the worldwide total.

Czar Alexander II of Russia

Alexander is generally regarded as one of the most enlightened rulers of Russia. He is noted for the emancipation of the serfs, peasants who lived almost like slaves, in 1861.

After the assassination of Czar Alexander II in March 1881 by a band of young revolutionaries, a rumor spread that the Jews were completely responsible. Because of the rumors, the Christian Russian majority conducted a series of pogroms—government-sanctioned acts of terrorism. Mobs invaded the shtetls, destroying Jewish homes and killing and wounding anyone unfortunate enough to cross their paths. These pogroms sparked a massive Jewish exodus. An estimated two million Russian Jews fled to the United States. Many more moved to Canada, Great Britain, and other countries. And some went to Palestine.

On August 2, 1492, Christopher Columbus glanced at some passing ships as he made final preparations for his famous voyage to the New World. "A fleet of misery and woe,"[7] he called them in his log.

Jews petition Ferdinand and Isabella for mercy, but a prelate holds the Christian cross in front of the monarchs in warning.

Those "woeful" ships contained the final Jews being expelled from Spain on the orders of Ferdinand and Isabella, the same monarchs who were paying for Columbus's voyage. For centuries, Spain had contained the largest and most prosperous Jewish population in Christian Europe. In 1391, thousands of Jews died in a series of persecutions. Many others became *conversos*, or converts to Christianity. The "traditional" Christian population, however, never completely trusted them.

In 1478, Ferdinand and Isabella instituted the Inquisition to ensure that converts practiced the Christian faith. *Conversos*—also called *marranos*, or swine—were a primary target. Many were publicly humiliated, subjected to torture, and burned alive.

The Spanish remained apprehensive, fearing that *conversos* would retain secret ties with those who remained Jewish. In March 1492, the monarchs issued the Edict of Expulsion, giving Jews four months to convert or leave. While up to 50,000 became *conversos*, the rest had to dispose of their property on short notice, in most cases not getting anywhere near its worth.

No one knows how many Jews left Spain under the harsh terms of the edict. Reliable estimates place the number at more than 200,000. Many crossed into Portugal, but their respite was only temporary. Four years later, Portuguese King Manoel forced nearly all to accept baptism on pain of death.

Perhaps the most fortunate fled to Muslim-controlled Turkey, where they received a warm welcome. Others went to North Africa or other parts of Europe. Some were sold into slavery. It seems likely that at least 20,000 perished. A number were thrown overboard by ship captains. Others were forced ashore in remote, inhospitable locations, where they soon died. Rumors even circulated that the refugees had swallowed valuable jewels. Bandits murdered many of them and sliced their stomachs open in a futile search for treasure.

Those who survived were known as the Sephardi Jews—they came from Christian Europe. The Jews who lived in Muslim-controlled Turkey and Africa became known as Ashkenazi.

Arthur Balfour had a career in the British government that spanned over five decades.

It began in 1874 when he was elected to Parliament at the age of 26 and lasted almost without interruption until just before his death in 1930. He was serving as foreign secretary when he issued the Balfour Declaration, which promised the Jews a homeland in Palestine.

The Balfour Declaration

In a sense, the arrival of fourteen Russian refugees in the Palestinian port of Jaffa in July 1882 marks the beginning of the nation of Israel. They—and thousands more who arrived during the following two decades—were the First Aliyah (ascent). Their goal was clear: "the political, national, and spiritual resurrection of the Jewish people in Palestine."[1]

During the previous century, a few thousand Jews had trickled into Palestine from Eastern Europe, mainly for religious reasons. Joining the small community of Jews already there, they became known as the Old Yishuv. They didn't particularly welcome the First Aliyah because of the secular orientation of the newcomers, who became known as the New Yishuv. Soon the New Yishuv would far outnumber the Old Yishuv, and the general name for the Jewish settlement would be known simply as the Yishuv.

Disagreements with the Old Yishuv weren't the First Aliyah's only obstacle in reaching their goal. For several centuries, Palestine had been controlled by the Muslim Ottoman Empire, which had neglected the area. Writer Mark Twain toured the region in 1868, noting that it was "a desolate country whose soil is rich enough, but is given over wholly to weeds—a silent mournful expanse. . . . A desolation is here that not even imagination can grace with the pomp of life and action. . . . There was hardly a tree or a shrub anywhere. Even the olive and the cactus, those fast friends of a worthless soil, had almost deserted the country."[2]

Another problem was reflected in a statement by an early settler named Israel Zangwill, who said Palestine was "a land without people for a people without land."[3] Zangwill was wrong. Several hundred thousand Arabs lived in Palestine and formed the vast majority of the population. For administrative purposes, Palestine was divided into several *vilayets,* or districts, whose borders changed periodically. The vilayets were in turn divided into several smaller units, or *sanjaks.* Because these areas were divided, there was no sense of a separate identity as

Jewish settlers of the First Aliyah.

It is likely that these settlers fled from the persecutions of Jews that followed the assassination of Czar Alexander II. Several of them wear the traditional Arab headdress.

Palestinian. Any nationalistic aspirations were bound up with Syria, a large swath of land from the Turkish border to the edge of Arabia that includes the modern-day nations of Syria, Lebanon, Israel, Kuwait, Jordan, and parts of Iraq.

Despite its status as a holy city to Jews, Christians, and Muslims, Jerusalem had undergone a steep population decline during Ottoman rule. "In the early 1840s, a British Admiralty survey estimated the population of Jerusalem at only twelve thousand,"[4] notes Professor Amiram Gonen. Within three decades, new neighborhoods—primarily Jewish—had sprouted up outside the walls of the Old City (historic Jerusalem), giving the city a Jewish majority. In 1889, the *Pittsburgh Dispatch* reported, "Thirty thousand out of 40,000 people in Jerusalem are Jews . . . at present the Jews are coming here by the hundreds."[5]

Though many of these "hundreds" were part of the First Aliyah, they did little toward establishing the Jews politically in Palestine. Discouraged by the harsh conditions they encountered, many left within a few years.

Then the vengeful French military decided to publicly humiliate Alfred Dreyfus, unwittingly setting off Herzl's crusade for a Jewish homeland. When the

First Zionist Congress was over, he wrote, "At Basel I founded the Jewish State. If I said this out loud today I would be greeted by universal laughter. Perhaps in five years, and certainly in 50, everyone will know it."[6] He proved remarkably prophetic; the State of Israel came into being about fifty years and eight months later.

At the time, however, many Jews opposed Zionism. Some objected on religious principles: They believed that Jews should not return to the Holy Land before the coming of the Messiah, the one anointed by God to provide peace and prosperity in their homeland. In this view, it was blasphemous for humans to try to accomplish that goal on their own. Others objected on practical grounds. They still held out hope for assimilation and feared the high profile Herzl had established could lead to retaliation.

Undeterred, Herzl plunged ahead. Knowing that Jews by themselves didn't have enough clout to establish their own state, he crisscrossed Europe and the Middle East in a tireless quest for support from the major powers. Despite his efforts, little happened for several years.

A renewed series of pogroms in Russia in April 1903 created chaos and panic, and once again many Jews fled. British colonial secretary Joseph Chamberlain offered land in Uganda, a British colony in Africa, for Jewish settlement. Herzl wanted to accept the offer on at least a temporary basis to deal with the emergency in Russia. Some Zionists bitterly criticized him, maintaining that their focus had to be exclusively on Palestine. Herzl died on July 3 the following year—before a homeland was established. He was just forty-four.

By then the pogroms had set off the Second Aliyah, which revived the ancient Hebrew language, established political parties, and laid the foundations for agricultural development. Many called themselves *sabras*, after the Hebrew word for prickly cactus, and established collective farms known as *kibbutzim*.

One of the estimated 40,000 people who came during this aliyah was a young Pole named David Gruen. He began working on a kibbutz and became active politically. Soon he changed his name to its Hebrew equivalent—David Ben-Gurion. Under this name, he would be included in *Time* magazine's list of the 100 most important people of the twentieth century.

In view of Ben-Gurion's future, his arrival in Palestine was ironic. The ship he was aboard anchored just offshore. As historian Benny Morris notes, "Porters carried the young Ben-Gurion to a skiff and then from a skiff to dry ground. He literally arrived in the Promised Land on the back of an Arab."[7]

By the time Ben-Gurion set foot in his new home, the Yishuv had purchased more than 15 percent of Palestine's land. The sellers included some of Palestine's most prominent Arab families, who took advantage of rising prices created by the new immigrants.

As Morris notes, "In some places the land was uninhabited; in others purchase led to the immediate eviction of Arab tenant farmers, many of whose families had themselves once been the proprietors. The fear of territorial displacement and dispossession was to be the chief motor of Arab antagonism to Zionism. . . . Neither the sellers nor the buyers were greatly concerned about the fate of the tenant farmers."[8]

Some didn't take the situation passively. As early as 1907, Jews began forming self-defense forces in response to Arab attacks. These attacks didn't deter further development. In 1909, a group of Jews stood on a barren sand dune and drew lots for building sites in what would become Tel Aviv. It was the first Jewish city to be established in more than 2,000 years.

Five years later, World War I broke out, and the British suddenly became very interested in Palestine. They desperately needed to retain control of the Suez Canal, which historian Barbara Tuchman terms "the hinge on which hung the British Empire."[9]

With the Ottoman Empire siding with Germany in the conflict, and thousands of Ottoman troops in Palestine only a short distance away from the canal, the region became a crucial focus of the British war effort. The British would say and do anything to advance their goal. Tuchman adds, "There was no clear [British] policy except to win the war and to emerge from it as firmly entrenched in the Middle East as possible."[10]

One element involved gaining the support of the Arabs. British diplomats promised them independence from Ottoman rule when the war ended.

The British also wanted Jewish support. In November 1917, British Foreign Secretary Arthur Balfour issued the Balfour Declaration, which would become a key document in the following three decades. It stated, in part: "His Majesty's Government view with favour the establishment in Palestine of a national home for the Jewish people and will use their best endeavours to facilitate the achievement of this object, it being clearly understood that nothing shall be done which may prejudice the civil and religious rights of existing non-Jewish communities in Palestine, or the rights and political status enjoyed by Jews in any other country."[11]

Professor Dawoud El-Alami, a native Palestinian, sums up a common response: "On what basis did the British believe that they were entitled to promise to the Zionists a land that belonged to others? This question lies at the core of the Palestinian position."[12]

Part of the answer comes from the Sykes-Picot Treaty, a secret agreement made between France and Britain in 1916 that divided the Middle East portions of the Ottoman Empire between them—assuming, of course, that they won the war. Palestine was part of the area the British would control. Palestine would be governed by an international body.

The treaty was made in secret because the British had publicly promised the Arabs that they would have independence; in private, they admitted they would not keep these promises. In addition, Tuchman notes a key provision in one of the written agreements between the British and Arabs: "Both the old Sherif Hussein and Feisal [the two primary Arab leaders] were cognizant [aware] of and

The treaty was drawn up by diplomats Mark Sykes of Britain and François Georges-Picot of France. When British troops conquered Palestine two years later, the region was added to Britain's area of control.

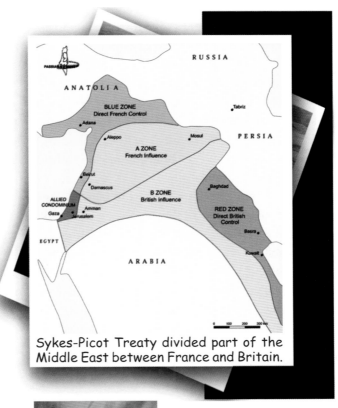

Sykes-Picot Treaty divided part of the Middle East between France and Britain.

acquiesced in [accepted] the exclusion of Palestine from the area of their promised independence, whether or not they had any mental reservations."[13]

In December, 1917, British troops—including thousands of Jewish volunteers—entered Jerusalem and ended four centuries of Ottoman occupation. Their efforts had been aided by Arab guerrillas, who kept large numbers of Ottoman soldiers busy in hit-and-run raids. The British assumed control of the rest of Palestine when World War I ended late in 1918.

Almost immediately the Third Aliyah began. In essence a continuation of the Second Aliyah—halted with the outbreak of the war—it brought another 40,000 Jews to Palestine. Nearly all were energetic young people who improved infrastructure with projects such as building roads and draining marshes to increase the amount of land available for farming.

British control became formalized in April 1920. The newly formed League of Nations established the British Mandate for Palestine. With League approval, the Balfour Declaration became an official part of the language of the Mandate.

Outraged, the Arabs began a series of riots which many commentators believe mark the birth of Palestinian nationalism. As Morris notes, "Early April 1920 had witnessed the crest of popular Arab belief in the idea of Palestine as part of an independent Greater Syria. By the end of April, the Palestinian leadership began to accept the country's separate identity."[14]

This leaning toward independence became even more pronounced the following year when Hajj Amin al-Husseini was appointed as Grand Mufti of Jerusalem. That made him the city's religious leader. Violently anti-British and anti-Jewish, he quietly began building up his influence and soon became the most powerful Arab in Palestine.

By then, the Jews had established a form of government for the Yishuv under the name of the Jewish Agency. Leaders began to emerge. One of the most important was Ben-Gurion. The Yishuv also established a defense force known as the Haganah (hah-guh-NAH, or "the defense").

In 1921, the British took the majority of Palestine—east of the Jordan River to the border with Iraq—and created a new mandate under the name of Transjordan. It was ruled by King Abdullah I.

Relations between the two sides continued to deteriorate as more Jews arrived between 1924 and 1929 in the Fourth Aliyah. The majority settled in cities. Tel Aviv experienced meteoric growth; the 1921 population of 4,000 swelled to 135,000 in fourteen years. Land purchases from the Arabs also continued.

The Jewish Legion consisted of several thousand volunteers who helped the British Army win battles in Palestine. Within a few years, Ben-Gurion would rise to a leadership position among the Jews in Palestine.

David Ben-Gurion served as a private in the Jewish Legion in 1918.

By 1929, the influx of some 75,000 Jews during the previous decade—doubling the overall Jewish population—prompted a renewed outbreak of Arab rioting. Hundreds of Jews were killed. The role of the Haganah began to expand significantly. In 1931, some members of the Haganah who wanted to be more aggressive broke off and formed the Irgun Bet.

Two years later, Nazi leader Adolf Hitler took control of the German government. Many German Jews recognized the danger that this dictator posed and began moving to Palestine. Within a few years, their numbers vastly increased the Fifth Aliyah—which had begun in 1929—and once again the Jewish population of Palestine doubled.

By then, Ben-Gurion had emerged as the unquestioned Jewish leader. He was elected as chairman of the Jewish Agency in 1935 and thereafter became the leading voice in Jewish politics.

Under the leadership of al-Husseini and the newly formed Arab Higher Committee, a general Arab strike began on April 15, 1936, and lasted for six months. Many on both sides were killed. Late that year the British government convened the Peel Commission to investigate the causes of the violence. It concluded that the there were too many issues on which the Arabs and Jews in Palestine could not agree. They presented a plan of partition as the only realistic solution. According to its proposal, each side would be given land based on the amount of the respective populations—the Arab portion was about three times larger—with a British-supervised corridor running from Jerusalem to the Mediterranean Sea.

Reluctantly the Jews accepted the plan. The Arabs refused, and rioting resumed. The British declared the Arab Higher Committee illegal. Though al-Husseini and other Arab leaders were forced into exile, the violence continued until early in 1939.

After the bloodshed, and realizing the danger that Hitler posed, the British reversed their policy. "The support of the Arab states and the Muslim world generally was much more crucial for Britain in the conflict with the Axis powers [Germany, Italy, and Japan] than the support of the Jews,"[15] observes historian Avi Shlaim.

In May, the British issued a White Paper, a document that reflected the official position of the British government. It stated: "His Majesty's government therefore now declares unequivocally that it is not part of their policy that Palestine should become a Jewish State."[16] The White Paper severely limited the amount of Jewish immigration and halted land purchases. It was a severe shock for the Yishuv, which now began to see the British as their enemy.

It was just as apparent that Hitler was also their enemy. Realizing their peril, many more Jews tried to leave Germany. The White Paper effectively removed Palestine as a place to go. Few countries were willing to accept the would-be refugees; the earlier havens of Britain and the United States now had very tight limits on Jewish immigration. To bypass those limits, President Franklin Roosevelt proposed opening up part of the Alaska Territory for Jewish settlement. Faced with vehement opposition from Alaskans, the proposal died in Congress in 1940.

By then, World War II had broken out. The rapid success of German armies soon put nearly all European Jews under Nazi control. Millions perished in the gas chambers of such notorious concentration camps as Dachau, Buchenwald, Treblinka, and Auschwitz in the Holocaust. Some died trying to avoid the Nazis. The tragic fate of the refugee ship *Struma* was a grim example of the risks of trying to flee Nazi genocide.

With Hitler's defeat in 1945, the surviving Jews may have thought their troubles were over. But they were still not completely free.

By September 1941, Romanian Jews knew their lives were in danger. Government officials in Romania, an ally of Nazi Germany, had already murdered thousands of Jews. According to historian Raul Hilberg, "no country, besides Germany, was involved in massacres of Jews on such a scale."[17] Consequently, nearly 800 people bought exorbitantly priced tickets for what was advertised as guaranteed admission to Palestine on a ship named the *Struma*.

The refugees must have been shocked when they saw the *Struma*. Built in 1830, it was 150 feet long and just 18 feet wide. It had only a single toilet.

The *Struma* departed on December 12. Within hours, the engine broke down. It was repaired, but failed again. Finally a tugboat towed the *Struma* into Istanbul, Turkey, where it anchored in the harbor. The passengers discovered that the promised entry to Palestine had been a hoax. The British refused to admit them and urged the Turks not to allow the ship to go any further. The Turks not only complied but also wouldn't allow any passengers to go ashore. They were marooned, with their only sustenance coming from local Jews who came up to the ship and handed food and water to them.

Adding to the difficulty, not everyone could be on deck at the same time. Hundreds had to stay below, enduring oppressive heat and smells. On February 23, 1942, the Turks forced them to leave, even though the engine still wasn't repaired. A tug towed the ship back into the Black Sea and turned it loose.

By midnight most of the passengers, including nineteen-year-old David Stoliar, were asleep. Several hours later Stoliar awoke to find himself tumbling through the air. He slammed into the frigid waters of the Black Sea. The *Struma* had disintegrated, almost certainly torpedoed by a Soviet submarine. Stoliar drifted for nearly twenty-four hours before a fishing boat plucked him from the icy water. He was the only survivor.

Nearly 230,000 Romanian Jews immigrated to Israel in the two decades following its independence—more than from any other European country.

David Stoliar

The *Exodus 1947* was a former American passenger vessel that sailed for Palestine in July 1947 with more than 4,500 Jews on board.

Nearly all were Holocaust survivors. British sailors boarded the ship while it was still in international waters, killed three people, and wounded dozens more. Then they forced the ship to return to Germany. The incident generated widespread publicity and helped convince the United Nations commission investigating the situation in Palestine to recommend partition.

CHAPTER 3

The Vote for Partition

Jews who had escaped the horrors of Hitler's concentration camps huddled in displaced persons camps and looked forward to a quick transit to Palestine. They quickly discovered that politics would pose a formidable barrier.

Britain's new prime minister, Ernest Bevin, wanted to cement his country's ties with the Arabs, largely to protect extensive oil interests in the region. He maintained the ban on Jewish immigration. Even though many Jews found space on Palestine-bound ships, the British Navy intercepted a number of these vessels and forced the passengers into prison camps on the island of Cyprus.

The Jewish Agency protested vigorously, appealing to the world for help and maintaining that the horrors of the Holocaust justified a state for them. Ben-Gurion took an active role. With the end of the war, a variety of surplus military equipment was being sold. He traveled to the United States and met with a group of wealthy American Jews who pledged their financial support to buy some of that equipment. This support was illegal, but that didn't deter Ben-Gurion's backers. What historian Dan Kurzman calls "one of the most effective and brilliantly operated underground operations in history"[1] generated tons of military gear for the Haganah. Ben-Gurion would later say that July 1, 1945 [the day of this meeting], "was the most important day in the history of Israel."[2]

One Jewish representative even contacted the Mafia, hoping to buy guns from them. The Mafia declined the deal, saying that the representative "didn't have an honest face."[3]

Back in Palestine, Jewish fighters participated in attacks against the British. The Irgun and another group, the Lehi (formed in 1940 and more extreme than the Irgun) took the lead. Professor Derek J. Penslar says starkly, "Lehi focused on murdering British soldiers."[4] Irgun was responsible for the most devastating attack, blowing up part of Jerusalem's King David Hotel in July 1946. Nearly 100 people—including 17 Jews—died in the blast.

In early 1947, the British decided that the effort to maintain the Mandate was too great, both in terms of money and human life. They turned it over to the United Nations, which established the United Nations Special Commission on Palestine (UNSCOP) to study the situation.

While the commission's members were in Palestine, they witnessed a dramatic incident involving the *Exodus 1947*, a ship crammed with Jewish refugees. The British turned it away. As historian Michael Oren notes, "The delegates were treated to a first-hand view of bayonet-wielding British troops herding more than forty-five hundred physically devastated but emotionally defiant survivors of Nazi death camps onto a boat back to Hamburg, Germany."[5]

Early in September UNSCOP issued its report, which called for partitioning Palestine into separate Jewish and Arab states. Jerusalem would be governed by an international commission. The proposed Arab state contained 4,500 square miles and a population of about 800,000 Arabs and 10,000 Jews. The Jewish state, of some 5,500 square miles, would hold just over half a million Jews and about 400,000 Arabs. While the larger size of the Jewish state might seem unfair, more than half consisted of the Negev Desert, where hardly anyone lived.

The proposed borders were a strategic nightmare. Each state would consist of three sections linked by two choke points—one in the Galilee region and the other west of Jerusalem—which could be easily blocked to seal off large portions of territory.

Jewish leaders were not sure whether the commission's plan would be accepted. They knew, however, that the key player would be U.S. president Harry Truman.

Truman faced a dilemma. The U.S. State Department vehemently opposed a Jewish state. Truman feared that the Arabs would overwhelm the Haganah if the Yishuv achieved statehood. Such a dire situation would force him to send up to 200,000 American troops to avert a wholesale massacre.

On the other hand, Jewish voters in the United States constituted a formidable bloc. And Truman was more than just a practical politician. As Penslar notes, "He had genuine sympathy for Zionism and a humanitarian concern for the misery of the Holocaust survivors."[6] Some of this sympathy came from what his personal representative, Earl G. Harrison, observed when he arrived in Europe soon after the war. Seeing American troops guarding emaciated Jewish concentration camp survivors, Robinson said, "We appear to be treating the Jews as the Nazis treated them, except that we do not exterminate them."[7]

As Truman struggled to make up his mind, Jewish leaders put immense pressure on him. Sometimes the pressure got to him. "Jesus Christ couldn't please them [the Jews] while he was here on this earth, so how would anyone expect that I would have any luck?"[8] he said on one occasion.

The Soviet Union forced his hand in mid-October by announcing its support for partition. By that time, the two countries—allies during World War II but rivals politically and economically ever since—were competing for influence around the world. Truman couldn't afford to allow the Soviets to gain the upper hand in the Middle East. He began an intense lobbying campaign among the uncommitted members of the United Nations.

The campaign was successful. The historic vote on November 29, 1947, was 33 in favor of partition, 13 opposed, and 10 abstentions—most notably the British. U.N. General Assembly Resolution 181 called for two independent states, one Arab and the other Jewish. The British mandate would end officially at midnight on May 15, 1948.

The Arab states were outraged and rejected the plan. However, one Arab leader didn't share this outrage—at least in private. The British had granted Transjordan its independence in 1946. By then, representatives of Transjordan's King Abdullah had been meeting secretly with the Jewish Agency. Abdullah didn't relish the prospect of having his political rival, the Grand Mufti Amin al-Husseini, in control of a state on his border. As authors Larry Collins and Dominique LaPierre explain, "A natural hatred had flourished between Abdullah and the Mufti of Jerusalem since their first meeting in 1921."[9]

Al-Husseini had spent the war years actively promoting the aims of Nazi Germany, and then returned to a tumultuous reception in Egypt. According to the Anglo-American Committee of Inquiry Regarding the Problems of European Jewry and Palestine, "He is probably the most popular Arab leader in Palestine."[10] Twelve days before the partition vote, Abdullah met with Golda Meir, a future Israeli prime minister.

"What would be your attitude be to an attempt by Transjordan to take control of the Arab part of Palestine?" he asked.

"We would view such action in a favorable light," she said, "especially if Your Majesty undertakes not to interfere with our efforts to set up a state."[11]

When the meeting broke up, Abdullah offered a final comment. "Don't pay any attention to my public statements." He grinned. "I have to make them, you know."[12]

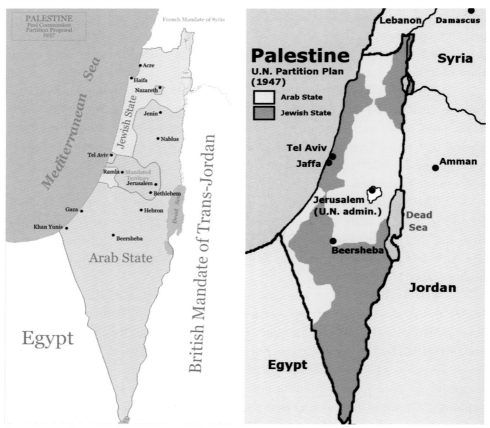

Two plans for partition. The Peel Commission (left) allotted a coastal strip and all of Galilee to the Jews. Eleven years later, the United Nations gave the same coastal strip to the Jews, divided Galilee, and added the Negev Desert in the south to Jewish territory.

Even without these assurances, one thing became immediately clear: Statehood would not come without a struggle.

Violence in Palestine broke out as soon as the results of the U.N. vote were announced. Both sides resorted to terror attacks, and Jews and Arabs alike began dying on an almost daily basis.

As the Jews would soon realize, it was one thing to have diplomats grant them independence. It would be another thing altogether to earn it. There would be no outside intervention to help enforce the terms of the resolution. The Yishuv was on its own.

When Germany surrendered in May 1945, the armed struggle in Europe came to an end. Immediately another struggle began—the struggle for survival. Millions of people had nowhere to go because their homes had been destroyed during six years of combat.

Three children in a displaced persons camp

These people soon acquired the name of displaced persons (DPs), and the victorious Allies established "displaced persons camps" to house and feed them. Most were set up in the American and British zones of occupied Germany; in a grim irony, a number of these facilities had been German concentration camps just a few months previously. Many of the inmates of DP camps were Jews who had somehow survived the horrors of Nazi tyranny. Once again they were surrounded by barbed wire and armed guards.

It wasn't just a matter of losing their homes and all or part of their families. In many cases, they were in DP camps because they weren't welcome in the countries from which they had been forcibly taken years earlier by the Germans. For example, mobs in Poland killed 46 returning Jews in July 1946. Similar incidents served to justify the conclusion of the Anglo-American Commission of Inquiry that same year: "It seems to them that the only real chance of rebuilding their shattered lives and of becoming normal men and women again is that offered in Palestine."[13]

With the British opposing this goal, many Jews faced a seemingly endless wait for release. They tried to live "normal" lives. They established governments, schools, newspapers, and theaters inside the camps. Sports were popular, with teams from different camps competing with each other.

Over the next few years, many nations opened their doors to DPs, Jews and non-Jews alike. Not surprisingly, Israel admitted the most—about 650,000—after achieving independence. After a relatively late start, the United States allowed 600,000, including a substantial number of Jews. Australia and Canada accepted about 350,000. Slowly the DP camps emptied, with the final one closing in 1957.

Members of the Haganah, the Jewish defense force, celebrate after breaking the Arab blockade of Jerusalem in mid-April 1948.

They enabled trucks carrying desperately needed food and ammunition to reach the beleaguered city. The respite proved to be only temporary. The Arabs soon reestablished control of the road leading to Jerusalem.

The End of the Mandate

The Arabs had attacked Jewish settlements all over Palestine as soon as the parition vote was announced. Jewish terrorists retaliated. The cycle of violence continued to escalate in 1948. Acting under Ben-Gurion's orders, the Haganah adopted a defensive role. Gurion didn't want to inflame world opinion against his soon-to-be country.

His strategy almost backfired. Even though they lacked effective leaders and sometimes acted more like a mob than a disciplined fighting body, the Arabs greatly outnumbered Jewish fighters. They slowly gained control of many roads that connected Jewish settlements. Often, the Arabs would occupy the high ground and fire down on Jewish convoys. Truck driver Yona Golani said, "I would become so frightened that the sweat would pour from my head down my neck. When you know that they could shoot at you from both sides, you'd hear a sort of echo inside, plucking at your nerves. It was also a horrible sight to see the car in front of you suddenly hit a mine and blow up. But you couldn't do a thing, only bite your lips. . . . You can cry, but you have to go on. The convoy must get through."[1]

March 1948 was especially difficult. The Haganah lost many vehicles and hundreds of men. The U.S. delegation to the United Nations was shocked by the violence. They began considering a plan that would delay the implementation of partition for an indefinite period of time. Meanwhile, an international group would oversee Palestine.

By the end of the month, the Arabs controlled the most important road in Palestine—the one linking Tel Aviv with Jerusalem. They had the power to deprive Jerusalem of the supplies it needed to survive. One of every six Jews in Palestine—about 100,000 people—lived there. Its loss would be catastrophic, especially on the symbolic level. A Jewish state without Jerusalem was unthinkable.

Buoyed by the arrival of new weapons from Czechoslovakia at the beginning of April, the Haganah became more aggressive. Operation Nachshon opened the Jerusalem road long enough to allow three convoys to reach the city.

By then, many Arabs had abandoned their homes. Some simply wanted to get away from the oncoming fighting and chaos. Arab leaders also called for Palestinians to flee, promising that they could return after the Arab victory. Others were forcibly expelled by Israeli soldiers. When Israeli soldiers massacred the villagers of Deir Yassin, still more Arabs fled.

To this day, there is disagreement as to how important each factor was. For example, *The Economist*, a respected British publication, commented, "Of the 62,000 Arabs who formerly lived in Haifa not more than 5,000 or 6,000 remained. Various factors influenced their decision to seek safety in flight. There is but little doubt that the most potent of the factors were the announcements made over the air by the Higher Arab Executive, urging the Arabs to quit [leave]."[2]

On the other hand, Ben-Gurion had said in 1938, "I support compulsory transfer. I do not see in it anything immoral."[3] And the Haganah's Plan D encouraged the "expulsion over the borders of the local Arab population in the event of opposition to our attacks."[4]

Whatever the reasons for Arab flight, it was welcome to the Jewish leadership. As Morris explained in a 2004 interview, "There could be no Jewish state with a large and hostile Arab minority in its midst. There would be no such state. It would not be able to exist."[5]

As the struggle continued, ten Jewish Agency leaders met on May 12, 1948, in Tel Aviv. On the table was a momentous motion: to declare independence. With the U.S. State Department still opposed to statehood, many American Jews urged they postpone making the decision for at least several weeks. The intense debate lasted until the following morning. Finally they voted: Six favored an immediate declaration, four opposed. Motion passed.

That led to another question. What would the new state be named?

One name was definitely off the table. "Palestine is a name the Romans gave to Eretz Yisrael with the express purpose of infuriating the Jews," said Golda Meir. "Why should we use the spiteful name meant to humiliate us?"[6]

Acceptable proposals included Zion, Jewish State, Judea, Land of Israel, and Yehuda. Ben-Gurion's suggestion of Israel was the winning choice.

Irgun and Lehi fighters attacked the village of Deir Yassin early on the morning of April 9, 1948. "What happened over the next few hours is still the subject of controversy and has, over the decades, become enveloped in lies and myths,"[7] notes author Anton La Guardia.

Attack on the village of Deir Yassin

Without doubt Arab civilians died during the assault. The controversy revolves around the number who were killed and the nature of their deaths.

Israeli combatants described the battle as fierce house-to-house combat and said that many if not most of the civilians—some of whom allegedly assisted Arab fighters—were killed by grenades exploding inside the houses. Arabs termed it a massacre, with unarmed women, children, and the elderly making up nearly all of the victims. Horrible stories—a number of them reported by non-Arabs—of rape, summary executions, and pregnant women being sliced open quickly appeared.

Historians generally concur with the "massacre" verdict. While there is general agreement today that just over 100 Arabs were killed, at the time the body count was inflated to more than 250. Morris notes, "Everyone had an interest in publicizing a high Arab casualty figure: the Haganah, to tarnish the [Irgun] and [Lehi]; the Arabs and British, to blacken the Jews; the [Irgun] and [Lehi], to provoke terror and frighten Arabs into fleeing the country."[8]

The Irgun and Lehi were unwittingly aided by the Arabs themselves. "The news of what happened—extensively covered and exaggerated in the Arab media for weeks—had a profoundly demoralizing effect on the Palestinian Arabs and was a major factor in their massive flight during the following weeks and months,"[9] Morris says. Collins and LaPierre concur, saying that Arab broadcasts of "the news of Deir Yassin in all its horror . . . stirred a growing sense of panic among the Arabs of Palestine."[10]

"Deir Yassin" also became a rallying cry among revenge-seeking Arabs who attacked a convoy of Jewish doctors, nurses, and patients four days later. The British refused to intervene, and ordered Israeli combatants to stay away. Only a handful of the 70 Israelis survived. The deadly spiral of violence continued.

Attack on the Jewish doctors, nurses, and patients as vengeance for Deir Yassin

Zion Gate was the scene of heavy fighting in May 1948.

Built in 1540, it was one of eight gates into the Old City of Jerusalem. Bullet scars attest to the intensity of the combat. Eventually the Arabs captured the Old City. Retaking it was one of the main goals of the Israeli Defense Force in the 1967 war.

The New Nation

On the afternoon of May 14, 1948, the day independence was formally declared, Rabbi Mordechai Weingarten heard a knock at the door of his small home in the Old City of Jerusalem. He opened it to see a British major.

"From [the major's] right hand dangled a bar of rusted iron almost a foot long," report Collins and LaPierre. "With a solemn gesture he offered it to the elderly rabbi. It was a key, the key to Zion Gate, one of the seven gates of the Old City of Jerusalem.

" 'From the year 70 A.D. until today,' he said, 'a key to the gates of Jerusalem has never been in Jewish hands. This is the first time in eighteen centuries that your people have been so privileged.' "[1]

At about the same time in Tel Aviv, a somber David Ben-Gurion stood beneath a portrait of Theodor Herzl and read the terms of the Jewish Declaration of Independence to dozens of equally somber delegates. They knew there were no assurances that the new nation would survive for more than a few weeks—or even a few days. Indeed, within twenty-four hours, troops from five neighboring Arab nations—Egypt, Transjordan, Lebanon, Syria and Iraq—poured into the newly declared state in an effort to overturn Ben-Gurion's declaration.

Yigal Allon, the Haganah chief of operations, said, "The regular forces of the neighbouring countries—with their equipment and their armaments—enjoy superiority at this time. . . . The problem is to what extent our men will be able to overcome enemy forces by virtue of their fighting spirit, of our planning and our tactics."[2] Many contemporary Israeli accounts depicted the struggle as a battle between the biblical David (Israel) and Goliath (the Arab states).

There is some support for this view. The Arabs had far more heavy equipment—tanks, artillery, airplanes. They could pick the areas they wanted to attack and concentrate superior force there. And they still controlled the high ground overlooking the Jerusalem road.

A portrait of Theodor Herzl is above Ben-Gurion, while the new nation's flag hangs to his left. The sober expressions on the listeners reveal their anxiety about what would come next.

David Ben-Gurion reads the Jewish Declaration of Independence.

Arab rhetoric reflected these advantages. One prominent Arab proclaimed, "This will be a war of extermination and a momentous massacre, which will be spoken of like the Mongolian massacres and the Crusades."[3] Another termed it "the elimination of the Jewish state."[4] A third added, "It does not matter how many [Jews] there are. We will sweep them into the sea."[5]

On the other hand, the number of Israelis under arms probably exceeded that of the Arab invaders. The Israelis were more disciplined, and their leadership was far superior. And they dominated, as Allon predicted, in "fighting spirit," or morale.

Another factor in the Israelis' favor was the Arabs' lack of overall coordination and—in the case of Transjordan—outright disagreement regarding their objectives. Morris notes, "The Arabs had done no proper planning or intelligence work, logistics were in a shambles, armaments and ammunition were in piteously short supply. Officers and soldiers alike were unprepared for what faced them."[6]

One optimistic Arab staff officer had developed a plan that called for an eleven-day campaign that would lead to victory. It fell apart almost immediately, largely because Abdullah decided that his top priority was occupying the West Bank (an area about 50 miles long and 20 miles wide on the west side of the Jordan River). In response, the Egyptian army changed its original plan, which had called for a powerful thrust up the coast to Tel Aviv, and diverted a substantial part of their forces toward the West Bank in an effort to get their "share." As Morris comments, "Thus the Arab war plan changed in conception and essence from a united effort to conquer parts of the nascent Jewish state and perhaps destroy it, into a multilateral land grab focusing on the Arab areas of the country."[7]

Nevertheless, the invaders made substantial inroads in the first week of the war. Hundreds of Israelis were killed or badly wounded in futile frontal assaults on Arabs controlling the Jerusalem road. The city's situation grew ever more critical. By June 5, the daily food ration was "150 grams [five ounces] a day—four thin slices—of a soggy, crumbling mass called bread, and, for a week, eight ounces of dried beans, peas and groats."[8]

Jerusalem's salvation came when David "Mickey" Marcus, a Jewish American military officer who had volunteered to help the new nation, pioneered a route that bypassed Arab strongpoints. Marcus's effort came too late to save the garrison in the Jewish Quarter. On May 28, the surviving defenders surrendered. The gate that had been symbolically opened to Weingarten just two weeks earlier slammed shut again.

"The shortest, saddest exile in modern Jewish history began just before sunset," explain Collins and LaPierre. "Two by two, some thirteen hundred residents of the Jewish Quarter started over the five hundred yards separating them from Zion Gate and the New City. Their departure marked the end of almost two thousand years of continuous Jewish residence . . . inside the Old Walls of Jerusalem."[9]

As the killing continued, the United Nations worked desperately on a cease-fire, which took effect on June 11. The delay benefited the Israelis, who had purchased immense stockpiles of arms in Europe. This equipment began pouring into Israel and decisively tipped the scales when fighting resumed.

The Israelis reopened the road to Jerusalem and advanced into areas assigned to the Arab state, most notably in the Upper Galilee, thereby removing the two choke points in the original partition plan and making their country easier to defend. Ben-Gurion even considered an attack on Abdullah's forces in the West Bank, but was persuaded not to.

By the end of the year, it was apparent that Israel had survived its birth pangs and established its independence. The cost was heavy. Many of the 6,000 who perished in less than a year and a half were buried at Mt. Herzl, the national cemetery, which "is full of graves without names. These are graves of Holocaust survivors who made it to Israel only to be handed a gun in order to fight for the survival of the Jewish nation. No one had time to get to know their names. They went down in history only as Yossi or Hershel or Moshe. It is a tragic thing to see all these graves marked 'Plony' ['John Doe']."[10]

While no one knows how many Arabs died, the numbers almost certainly were much higher than Jewish losses. To Arabs, the outcome "was the *nakba*, the Disaster: banishment from their ancestral homes as the innocent victims of aggressive Jewish nationalism."[11]

Early in 1949, U.N. diplomat Ralph Bunche called together a peace conference on the Greek island of Rhodes. A series of armistice agreements ended the fighting. For his efforts, Bunche was awarded the Nobel Peace Prize.

Israelis celebrate a new settlement in Western Galilee early in 1949.

Western Galilee was one of the areas assigned to Arabs under the U.N. partition plan (see map on page 28). Capturing Western Galilee not only added more land to Israel, but also made the new nation's borders easier to defend.

Twenty-thousand marchers and thousands of others took part in the parade, including Israel's labor unions and cooperative organizations. The float represents farming on the Kibbutzim.

Israel had its first May Day Parade on May 1, 1949.

Bunche's skill, however, couldn't solve the problem created by an estimated 700,000 Palestinian Arabs who no longer had their homes. About two-thirds were in the Gaza Strip and the West Bank, the remaining Arab-controlled areas of the U.N. partition plan. Many have lived there ever since. Their situation has generated a great deal of sympathy through the years.

Much less known is what happened to a similar number of Jewish refugees. A headline in the *New York Times* on May 16, 1948, declared, "Jews in Grave Danger in All Moslem Lands: Nine Hundred Thousand in Africa and Asia Face Wrath of Their Foes."[12]

The results of this wrath soon became evident. While relatively few were actually forced to abandon their communities—some of which had flourished for up to 2,500 years—"the fierce hostility to Jews throughout the Arab world generated by the first Arab-Israeli war drove Jews to emigrate in large numbers," notes Professor Bernard Wasserstein. "In many Arab countries, anti-Jewish riots accelerated the exodus."[13]

President Harry Truman (left) congratulates Ralph Bunche.

Truman awarded Bunche the Outstanding Citizenship Award on November 15, 1949. Bunche had successfully negotiated a cease-fire between the Arabs and Israelis earlier in the year. At the time, he was one of the highest-ranking African-Americans in the U.S. government.

Over a period of several years, nearly all who left the Arab lands came to Israel. Coupled with European immigration, Israel doubled its population in the three years following its establishment as it fulfilled Herzl's vision of a Jewish homeland—at least in part. Several generations of Israelis have lived "as free men [and women] on our own soil," as he wrote more than a century ago. But his wish that Jews could "die peacefully in our own fatherland" remains unrealized.

Israel has never known true peace. "The armistice agreements were not followed by peace treaties," Wasserstein says. "Israel was regarded as a pariah by all the Arab states."[14]

During the 1949 negotiations, Mahmoud Riad, who later became Egyptian foreign minister, said, "We cannot accept you [Israel]. . . . [To] make peace with you would mean that we have to accept that you are here to stay. We are not ready. This situation in our country and in the Arab world will not permit it. We cannot yet live in peace with you."[15]

These words could just have easily been written nearly six decades later.

U.N. Resolution 181 called for the establishment of two states in Palestine, one for Jews, one for Arabs. Yet no viable Palestinian Arab state came into existence at that time—or since then.

In September 1948, an All-Palestine government was declared with headquarters in the Gaza Strip. On October 1, it declared itself the government of all of Palestine even though Israeli forces controlled most of the country. Nevertheless, six of the seven Arab states that had declared war on Israel—Egypt, Syria, Lebanon, Iraq, Saudi Arabia, and Yemen—immediately recognized it. Transjordan didn't, nor did any non-Arab country. After the armistice between Egypt and Israel the following February, this government stopped functioning and was formally disbanded three years later.

Transjordanian forces occupied the West Bank during the fighting with Israel and remained there following the armistice. A similar situation prevailed in Gaza, with Egyptian troops controlling the area from which they had launched their invasion the previous May. Neither occupier made an effort to establish a Palestinian state. Jordan (the name by which Transjordan became known) formally annexed the West Bank and East Jerusalem in 1950, giving Palestinians full Jordanian citizenship.

There was little opposition among Palestinians to Jordanian or Egyptian control. The most overt act of resistance occurred in 1951, when a Palestinian who believed Abdullah was about to conclude a peace treaty with Israel assassinated the monarch.

As Professor Jamal R. Nassar explains, "In the period immediately following their diaspora, Palestinian intellectuals believed that the remedy for their plight rested on Arab unity. . . . Palestinians at this early stage looked for help from the Arab governments."[16]

The situation changed in 1967, when Israel captured the West Bank, East Jerusalem, and Gaza during the Six-Day War. Faced with occupation by Israelis rather than Arabs, Palestinians began demanding autonomy.

Nassar continues, "More than a third of the Palestinians were now faced with the enemy as their occupying master. . . . Palestinian nationalism began to replace the traditional Arab nationalism which had dominated Palestinian political culture prior to 1967."[17]

Despite decades of diplomatic efforts, the quest for a Palestinian state remains unfulfilled.

Paratroopers at the Western Wall after the Six-Day War

Chronology

BCE*

1850	Abraham journeys to Canaan [the modern-day Holy Land], believing God has promised that he will found a great nation.
1700	Jews move to Egypt and eventually become enslaved.
1250	Jews flee from Egypt under the leadership of Moses.
1050	The Kingdom of Israel is founded.
1004–965	Reign of King David, who captures Jerusalem and makes the city the capital of Israel.
960	David's son Solomon builds the First Temple in Jerusalem.
931	Israel is divided into Israel and Judah.
721	Assyrian King Sargon II captures Israel.
586	Babylonians under Nebuchadnezzar capture Judah and Jerusalem, destroy the temple, and force Jews to go to Babylon.
538	Persian King Cyrus captures Babylon and allows Jews to return to Jerusalem.
536	Construction begins on Second Temple.
166	Revolt led by Judas Maccabee leads to Jewish independence.
63	Romans take control of what is now called Judea.

CE

66–70	Jews revolt against Roman rule; Second Temple is destroyed, leaving only the Western Wall.
132–135	Jews revolt; Diaspora begins; Judea is renamed Syria Palestina.
610–632	Muhammad founds the religion of Islam.
638	Caliph Umar declares that Muhammad ascended to heaven from Jerusalem, making the city the third-most holy site in Islam.
1099	Christians in First Crusade capture Jerusalem and slaughter most of its Jewish and Muslim population.
1187	Muslim leader Saladin recaptures Jerusalem and expels the Crusaders.
1492	After instituting the Inquisition in 1478, Spain expels nearly all of its Jewish population.
1611	The word "ghetto" appears for the first time.
1791	Catherine the Great establishes the Pale of Settlement in Russia.
1881	The assassination of Czar Alexander II in Russia leads to pogroms against Jews and sparks a massive Jewish exodus from Russia.
1882	The First Aliyah begins.
1886	David Ben-Gurion is born.
1894	French army officer Alfred Dreyfus, who is Jewish, is wrongly convicted of espionage.
1895	Theodor Herzl founds Zionist movement.
1897	The First Zionist Congress convenes in Basel, Switzerland.
1903	The Second Aliyah begins.
1904	Theodor Herzl dies.
1909	Tel Aviv is founded.
1917	British Foreign Secretary Arthur Balfour expresses support for a Jewish homeland in the Balfour Declaration.
1919	The Third Aliyah begins soon after the end of World War I the previous November.
1920	The League of Nations grants the British a mandate over Palestine.
1921	The British create a separate mandate for Transjordan; Hajj Amin al-Husseini becomes Grand Mufti of Jerusalem.
1924	The Fourth Aliyah begins.
1929	The Fifth Aliyah begins.
1933	Adolf Hitler becomes German dictator; first concentration camp is established at Dachau, Germany. More Jews join the Fifth Aliyah.
1936	Palestinian Arabs begin general strike, which soon turns violent; sporadic fighting continues for three years.

1937	Peel Commission recommends partition.
1939	British issue White Paper that severely curtails further Jewish immigration; World War II begins when Germany invades Poland.
1942	The refugee ship *Struma* explodes in the Black Sea after the British refuse to allow it to continue to Palestine. More than 700 Jews die.
1945	World War II in Europe ends; homeless Jews and others begin entering displaced persons camps.
1947	United Nations Special Commission on Palestine (UNSCOP) is established; the U.N. General Assembly votes to partition Palestine into two states; conflict between Arabs and Jews in Palestine begins.
1948	Israel declares its independence. Ben-Gurion becomes its first prime minister. Israel defeats invading armies from five Arab countries.
1949	Chaim Weizmann is elected Israel's first President; Israel signs armistice agreements with the countries that attacked it.
1956	Egypt nationalizes the Suez Canal; Israeli armies, under secret pact with Britain and France, invade the Sinai Peninsula but are soon forced to withdraw.
1964	Arab League founds the Palestine Liberation Organization (PLO), with the stated goal of destroying Israel.
1967	Israel defeats several Arab nations in the Six-Day War and more than doubles its size, primarily by capturing the Sinai Peninsula.
1968	Israel begins building settlements in territory captured during the Six-Day War.
1969	Golda Meir becomes Israeli prime minister. Yasser Arafat is elected chairman of PLO's executive committee.
1972	Black September terrorists murder eleven Israeli athletes at the Munich Olympic Games.
1973	Following initial reverses after being attacked by Syria and Egypt, Israel wins the Yom Kippur War; Ben-Gurion dies.
1978	The Camp David Accords lead to diplomatic recognition of Israel by Egypt and return of the Sinai Peninsula to Egypt.
1982	Israel invades Lebanon; when Lebanese president-elect Bashir Gemayel is assassinated, Christians massacre hundreds of Palestinans in two refugee camps in retaliation.
1987	The First Intifada (uprising) breaks out in Gaza; it lasts until 1990 and draws international attention to Palestinian demands for independence.
1993	Israel and PLO agree to mutual recognition and transition to Palestinian self-rule in the West Bank and Gaza Strip in the Oslo Accords. Negative publicity from both sides prevents them from reaching their goals.
1995	Israeli Prime Minister Yitzhak Rabin, one architect of the Oslo Accords, is assassinated by an Israeli extremist. His successor, Shimon Peres, is defeated the following May by Benjamin Netanyahu, who opposes the agreement.
1996	PLO formally revokes all clauses in its founding charter calling for the dissolution of Israel.
2000	The Second Intifada begins.
2004	Yasser Arafat dies.
2005	World leaders and concentration camp survivors meet at Auschwitz on January 27 to mark the sixtieth anniversary of the liberation of the most notorious Nazi death camp during the Holocaust. (At least 1.5 million Jews, Gypsies, Poles, Catholics, homosexuals, and Soviet POWs died there.)
2006	Iranian President Mahmoud Ahmadinejad labels the Holocaust a "myth" and calls for the elimination of Israel; Israel attacks Lebanon after Palestinian guerrillas based there kidnap two Israeli soldiers.
2007	Palestinian factions Hamas and Fatah fight each other; Fatah controls the West Bank, and Hamas is in control in the Gaza Strip.

*Some early dates are approximations.

Chapter Notes

Chapter 1 The Birth of Zionism

1. Chronology of the Dreyfus Affair, http://www.georgetown.edu/faculty/guieuj/ DreyfusCase/Chronology%20of%20the%20 Dreyfus%20Affair.htm

2. Frederick Painton, "A Century Late, the Truth Arrives: The French Army Concedes That Alfred Dreyfus Was Innocent," *Time*, September 25, 1995, http://www.time.com/time/ international/1995/950925/history.html

3. Trent Hawthorne, "Theodore Herzl and the Dreyfus Trial," http://www.ccds. charlotte.nc.us/History/MidEast/save/ hawthorne/hawthorne.htm

4. Ibid.

5. Gideon Shimoni, "Historiographical Issues in Conveying Herzl's Legacy," http:// www.wzo.org.il/en/resources/view.asp?id=2119

6. Howard Sachar, *A History of the Jews in the Modern World* (New York: Alfred A. Knopf, 2005), p. 4.

7. Ibid., p. 138.

Chapter 2 The Balfour Declaration

1. The First Aliyah (1882–1903), http:// www.jewishvirtuallibrary.org/jsource/ Immigration/First_Aliyah.html

2. Ottoman Rule on the Eve of World War I, http://www.jafi.org.il/education/100/maps/ ottoman.html

3. Muhammad Hallaj, "From Time Immemorial: The Resurrection of a Myth," http://www.ameu.org/page.asp?iid=114& aid=156&pg=1

4. Amiram Gonen, *Israel Yesterday and Today: A Photographic Survey of the Building of a Nation* (New York: Macmillan USA, 1998), p. 13.

5. *The Pittsburgh Dispatch*, July 15, 1889, http://www.infoisrael.net/cgi-local/text.pl? source=3/e/230620031

6. Bernard Reich, *A Brief History of Israel* (New York: Facts on File, 2005), p. 17.

7. Benny Morris, *Righteous Victims: A History of the Zionist–Arab Conflict, 1881–1999* (New York: Alfred A. Knopf, 1999), p. 45.

8. Ibid., pp. 37–38.

9. Barbara Tuchman, *Bible and Sword: England and Palestine from the Bronze Age to Balfour* (New York: Ballantine Books, 1984), p. 319.

10. Ibid., p. 320.

11. Ibid., p. 339.

12. Dan Cohn-Sherbock and Dawoud el-Alami, *The Palestine–Israeli Conflict: A Beginner's Guide* (Oxford, Great Britain: One World Publications, 2002), p. 104.

13. Tuchman, p. 329.

14. Morris, p. 99.

15. Avi Shlaim, *The Iron Wall: Israel and the Arab World* (New York: W.W. Norton, 2001), p. 22.

16. Amos Perlmutter, *Israel, the Partitioned State: A Political History Since 1900* (New York: Charles Scribner's Sons, 1985), p. 76.

17. Douglas Frantz and Catherine Collins, *Death on the Black Sea: The Untold Story of the Struma and World War II's Holocaust at Sea* (New York: HarperCollins, 2003), p. 33.

Chapter 3 The Vote for Partition

1. Dan Kurzman, *Genesis 1948: The First Arab Israeli War* (New York: New American Library, 1970), p. 107.

2. Bernard Postal and Henry W. Levy, *And the Hills Shouted for Joy: The Day Israel Was Born* (New York: David McKay, 1973), p. 194.

3. Kurzman, p. 108.

4. Derek J. Penslar, "To Be a Free Nation," in Nicholas de Lange (editor), *The Illustrated History of the Jewish People* (New York: Harcourt Brace and Company, 1997), p. 347.

5. Michael B. Oren, *Power, Faith, and Fantasy: American in the Middle East, 1776 to the Present* (New York: W. W. Norton, 2007), p. 490.

6. Penslar, p. 347.

7. Oren, p. 495.

8. Ibid., p. 488.

9. Larry Collins and Dominique LaPierre, *O Jerusalem!* (New York: Simon and Schuster, 1972), p. 82.

10. Anne Sinai and I. Robert Sinai (editors), *Israel and the Arabs: Prelude to the Jewish State* (New York: Facts on File, 1972), p. 52.

11. Kurzman, *Genesis 1948: The First Arab Israeli War* (New York: New American Library, 1970), pp. 23–24.

12. Ibid., p. 24.

13. Sinai and Sinai, p. 46.

Chapter 4 The End of the Mandate

1. March of the Living International 2002: Chapter XVI. The War of Independence (1947–1949), http://www.motl.org/resource/curriculum/curriculum_16.htm

2. "The Palestinian Refugee Issue," http://zionism-israel.com/issues/Zionism_Israel_Wujs_refugees.html

3. Benny Morris, *Righteous Victims: A History of the Zionist–Arab Conflict, 1881–1999* (New York: Alfred A. Knopf, 1999), p. 253.

4. Simha Flapan, *The Birth of Israel* (New York: Pantheon Books, 1987), p. 42.

5. Ari Shavit Haaretz, "Survival of the Fittest (an interview with Historian Benny Morris)," January 9, 2004, http://www.deiryassin.org/bennymorris.html

6. The History and Meaning of "Palestine" and "Palestinian," http://www.tzemach.org/fyi/docs/speak/nopal.htm

7. Anton La Guardia, *War Without End: Israelis, Palestinians, and the Struggle for a Promised Land* (New York: St. Martin's Press, 2001), p. 196.

8. Morris, p. 209.

9. Ibid.

10. Larry Collins and Dominique LaPierre, *O Jerusalem!* (New York: Simon and Schuster, 1972), p. 281.

Chapter 5 The New Nation

1. Larry Collins and Dominique LaPierre, *O Jerusalem!* (New York: Simon and Schuster, 1972), p. 10.

2. Martin Gilbert, *The Routledge Atlas of the Arab-Israeli Conflict*. Seventh edition (New York: Routledge, 2002), p. 46.

3. Benny Morris, *Righteous Victims: A History of the Zionist–Arab Conflict, 1881–1999* (New York: Alfred A. Knopf, 1999), p. 219.

4. Ibid.

5. Ibid.

6. Ibid.

7. Ibid., p. 221.

8. Collins and LaPierre, p. 524.

9. Ibid., p. 499.

10. "Independence Day," http://www.ajudaica.com/Jewish_holidays/48

11. "Israeli and Palestinian History: So Hard to Reconcile," *The Economist*, March 15, 2007, http://www.economist.com/world/international/displaystory.cfm?story_id=8859085

12. United Nations Economic and Social Council, Historical Facts and Figures: The Forgotten Jewish Refugees from Arab Countries, March 17, 2003, http://domino.un.org/unispal.nsf/eed216406b50bf6485256ce10072f637/fe7989175118cda585256d750050cbc9!OpenDocument

13. Bernard Wasserstein, "The Age of Upheavals," in Nicholas de Lange (editor), *The Illustrated History of the Jewish People* (New York: Harcourt Brace and Company, 1997), pp. 359–360.

14. Ibid., p. 358.

15. Dan Cohn-Sherbock and Dawoud el-Alami. *The Palestine–Israeli Conflict: A Beginner's Guide* (Oxford, Great Britain: One World Publications, 2002), p. 138.

16. Jamal R. Nassar, "The Culture of Resistance: The 1967 War in the Context of the Palestinian Struggle—Israeli-Arab War of 1967; Palestinian Displacement by Creation of Israel," *Arab Studies Quarterly*, Summer, 1997, http://findarticles.com/p/articles/mi_m2501/is_n3_v19/ai_20755836/pg_1

17. Ibid.

Glossary

annexed (AA-nekst)—added as part of a larger country or state.

anti-Semitism (an-tee-SEH-meh-tism)—hatred (in thoughts, words, or actions) toward Jewish people.

assimilation (uh-sih-muh-LAY-shun)—living and working peaceably with another culture.

bloc (BLOK)—a group of people or nations that act together to achieve a common goal.

debasing (dee-BAY-sing)—lowering in status, humiliating.

dispossession (dis-poh-SEH-shun)—the loss of one's home, property, and security.

exodus (EK-suh-dus)—mass departure.

genocide (JEH-nuh-cide)—systematic destruction of a population or cultural group, usually with government assistance.

imperialism (im-PEER-ee-ul-ism)—extending the power of a nation by controlling other nations or territories.

infrastructure (IN-fruh-struk-chur)—basic framework; system of public works including roads, sewers, buildings, communication systems, and other elements essential for a society to function.

mufti (MOOF-tee)—a professional judge who interprets Muslim law.

multilateral (mul-ty-LAA-tur-ul)—many-sided; involving at least two nations.

orientation (or-ee-un-TAY-shun)—leaning; direction.

pariah (puh-RY-uh)—outcast; one that is despised.

pogrom (pah-GROM)—government-approved persecution of a group.

rabbi (RAA-by)—a teacher of Judaism.

secular (SEH-kyoo-lur)—having to do with worldly pursuits, rather than spiritual ones.

shtetl (SHTAY-tul)—one of the many impoverished Jewish villages in the Pale of Settlement, Russia.

sundered (SUN-derd)—broke apart.

Further Reading

For Young Adults

Bard, Mitchell (editor). *At Issue in History: The Founding of the State of Israel.* San Diego, California: Greenhaven Press, 2003.

Goldstein, Margaret J. *Israel in Pictures.* Minneapolis, Minnesota: Lerner Publications Group, 2004.

Greenfeld, Howard. *A Promise Fulfilled: Theodor Herzl, Chaim Weizmann, David Ben-Gurion, and the Creation of the State of Israel.* New York: Greenwillow, 2005

Harris, Nathaniel. *Israel and the Arab Nations in Conflict.* Chicago: Raintree, 1999.

Katz, Samuel M. *Jerusalem or Death: Palestinian Terrorism.* Minneapolis, Minnesota: Lerner Publishing Group, 2003.

Minnis, Ivan. *The Arab-Israeli Conflict.* Chicago: Raintree, 2003.

Works Consulted

Cohn-Sherbock, Dan, and Dawoud el-Alami. *The Palestine–Israeli Conflict: A Beginner's Guide.* Oxford, Great Britain: One World Publications, 2002.

Collins, Larry, and Dominique LaPierre. *O Jerusalem!* New York: Simon and Schuster, 1972.

De Lange, Nicholas (editor). *The Illustrated History of the Jewish People.* New York: Harcourt Brace and Company, 1997.

Flapan, Simha. *The Birth of Israel.* New York: Pantheon Books, 1987.

Frantz, Douglas, and Catherine Collins. *Death on the Black Sea: The Untold Story of the Struma and World War II's Holocaust at Sea.* New York: HarperCollins, 2003.

Gilbert, Martin. *The Routledge Atlas of the Arab-Israeli Conflict*. Seventh edition. New York: Routledge, 2002.

Gonen, Amiram. *Israel Yesterday and Today: A Photographic Survey of the Building of a Nation*. New York: Macmillan USA, 1998.

Kurzman, Dan. *Genesis 1948: The First Arab Israeli War*. New York: New American Library, 1970.

La Guardia, Anton. *War Without End: Israelis, Palestinians, and the Struggle for a Promised Land*. New York: St. Martin's Press, 2001.

Morris, Benny. *Righteous Victims: A History of the Zionist–Arab Conflict, 1881–1999*. New York: Alfred A. Knopf, 1999.

Oren, Michael B. *Power, Faith, and Fantasy: American in the Middle East, 1776 to the Present*. New York: W. W. Norton, 2007.

Perlmutter, Amos. *Israel, the Partitioned State: A Political History Since 1900*. New York: Charles Scribner's Sons, 1985.

Postal, Bernard, and Henry W. Levy. *And the Hills Shouted for Joy: The Day Israel Was Born*. New York: David McKay, 1973.

Reich, Bernard. *A Brief History of Israel*. New York: Facts on File, 2005.

Sachar, Howard. *A History of the Jews in the Modern World*. New York: Alfred A. Knopf, 2005.

Shlaim, Avi. *The Iron Wall: Israel and the Arab World*. New York: W.W. Norton, 2001.

Sinai, Anne, and I. Robert Sinai (editors). *Israel and the Arabs: Prelude to the Jewish State*. New York: Facts on File, 1972.

Tuchman, Barbara. *Bible and Sword: England and Palestine from the Bronze Age to Balfour*. New York: Ballantine Books, 1984.

On the Internet

Chronology of the Dreyfus Affair http://www9.georgetown.edu/faculty/guieuj/DreyfusCase/Chronology%20of%20the%20Dreyfus%20Affair.htm

The First Aliyah (1882–1903) http://www.jewishvirtuallibrary.org/jsource/Immigration/First_Aliyah.html

Haaretz, Ari Shavit. "Survival of the Fittest (An interview with historian Benny Morris)," January 9, 2004. http://www.deiryassin.org/bennymorris.html

Hallaj, Muhammad. "From Time Immemorial: The Resurrection of a Myth." http://www.ameu.org/page.asp?iid=114&aid=156&pg=1

Hawthorne, Trent. "Theodore Herzl and the Dreyfus Trial." http://www.ccds.charlotte.nc.us/History/MidEast/save/hawthorne/hawthorne.htm

The History and Meaning of "Palestine" and "Palestinian." http://www.tzemach.org/fyi/docs/speak/nopal.htm

Holocaust Encyclopedia: Displaced Persons http://www.ushmm.org/wlc/article.php?lang=en&ModuleId=10005462

Israel Defense Forces—The Official Website. http://dover.idf.il/IDF/English/

"Israeli and Palestinian History: So Hard to Reconcile." *The Economist*, March 15, 2007. http://www.economist.com/world/international/displaystory.cfm?story_id=8859085

Jewish Refugees http://www.pushhamburger.com/july_pearl.htm

Kaplan, Jonathan. "The Origins of Israeli Society: Formative Groups and Ideologies." http://www.jewishagency.org/JewishAgency/English/Home

Kleiman, Shelley. "The State of Israel Declares Independence." http://www.mfa.gov.il/MFA

March of the Living International 2002: Chapter XVI. The War of Independence (1947–1949) http://www.motl.org/resource/curriculum/curriculum_16.htm

Nassar, Jamal R. "The Culture of Resistance: The 1967 War in the Context of the Palestinian Struggle—Israeli-Arab War of 1967; Palestinian Displacement by Creation of Israel," *Arab Studies Quarterly*, Summer, 1997. http://findarticles.com/p/articles/mi_m2501/is_n3_v19/ai_20755836/pg_1

Ottoman Rule on the Eve of World War I http://www.jafi.org.il/education/100/maps/ottoman.html

Painton, Frederick. "A Century Late, the Truth Arrives: The French Army Concedes That Alfred Dreyfus Was Innocent." *Time*, September 25, 1995. http://www.time.com/time/international/1995/950925/history.html

Palestine Facts http://www.palestinefacts.org/pf_mandate_oppose_immigration.php

Palestine/Israel http://www.ajzenberg.com/Book/185.htm

Index